Welcome to Vocabulary Power

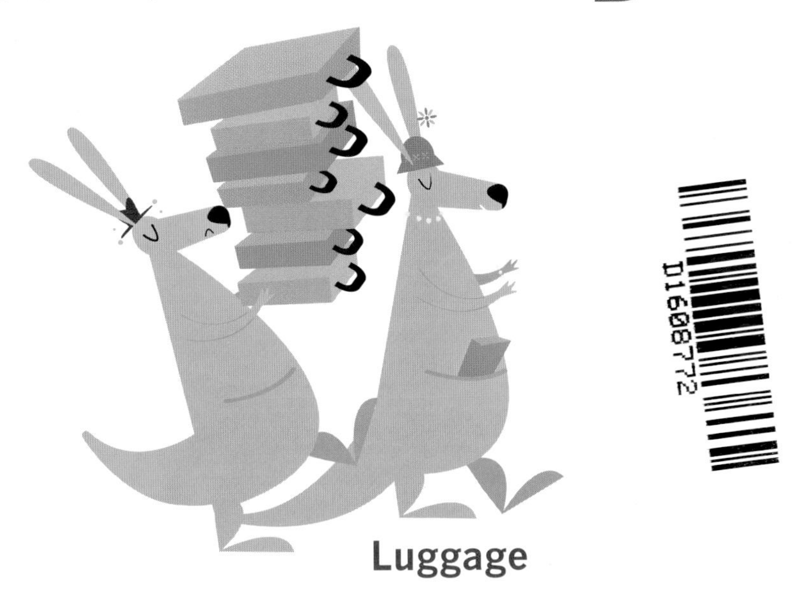

D16008772

Luggage is what you carry your things in when you travel.

Make it fun!

- Read a word every day with your child. Make it a special time that you both look forward to. At breakfast or before bed, a few minutes a day will make a lifetime of difference in your child's education.
- Look at the illustration. How does it show the meaning of the word? Ask your child to brainstorm another way to express the same idea in a picture.
- Read the question at the bottom of the page. Can you or your child guess the answer? Use the word in a question, sentence, or riddle of your own.
- Encourage your child to use each new word at least three times during the next day.

Context Is Everything

- Literacy experts agree that developing early vocabulary is the key to future learning. A deficiency in vocabulary as early as third grade can prove virtually insurmountable in later life.
- Research shows that children with a strong vocabulary do better in school and move joyfully along the road to academic success.
- A child with a strong vocabulary is not only a better reader, but also benefits from greater self-esteem. Confident kids are happy kids!

Where These 200 Words Come From

Kids love learning the meaning of words that they encounter in their favorite books. We compiled our 200 words from the world's most popular and beloved children's literature. Educators regard our word collection as a key component for developing a child's vocabulary.

The Team

AUTHOR, Audrey Carangelo has twenty years' experience developing language arts, reading, and phonics curricula used in classrooms nationwide. She has written dozens of books for beginning readers.

SPECIAL THANKS to the wonderful involvement of Catherine Rupf, Anne Burrus, Frédéric Michaud, Audrey Carangelo, Adrienne Schure, Joe and Denise Kiernan, and the great team of the Bill SMITH STUDIO.

BY THE SAME PUBLISHER

HOMEWORK

Helpster™

TimeLine™

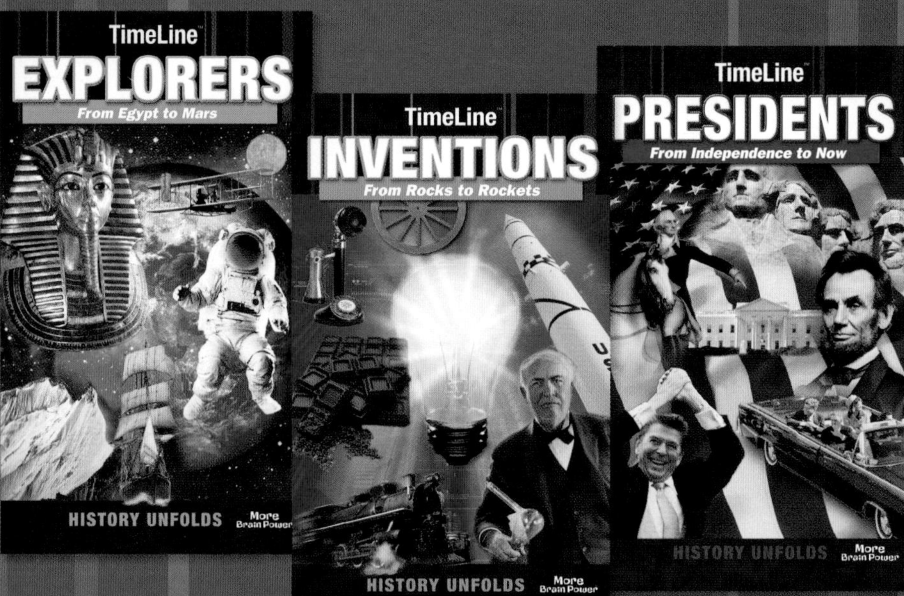
TimeLine™
EXPLORERS
From Egypt to Mars
HISTORY UNFOLDS
More Brain Power
TimeLine™
INVENTIONS
From Rocks to Rockets
HISTORY UNFOLDS
More Brain Power
TimeLine™
PRESIDENTS
From Independence to Now
HISTORY UNFOLDS
More Brain Power

Pronunciation Guide

Vowels

a	cat
ah	father, car, pot
ay	say, tame, paid, pair, scare
aw	law, caught
e	bet, send
ee	meet, seat, ear
i	fit
ie	pie, bite, eye, sigh
oh	so, slow, bone
oo	school, pool
or	born, score
oi	boil, coin, boy
ow	cow, mouth
u	cook, put
uh	fun, action, soda, about, trouble, travel
ur	curve, nerve, better
yoo	mule

Consonants

b	book, bear
ch	match, chop
d	dog, bed
f	fit, cliff, phone
g	got, bag
h	how, whole
j	jar, germ, badge
k	cat, quit, keep, sock
l	let, tall
m	mad, lamb
n	no, ten, know
ng	song
p	pen, sip
r	ribbon, car
s	sat, rice, class
sh	shape, rush
t	tell, bat
th	thin, both
th	the, breathe
v	vine, save
w	will, white
y	you
z	zap
zh	treasure

Available in the Series

Enormous

(i – **NOR** – muhs) *adjective*

Something that is very, very large is enormous.

? Can a mountain be enormous?

! Yes. Mountains can be very big.

Snack

(**SNAK**) *noun*

A snack is a quick, simple meal.

? Which is a snack: an apple, or a turkey dinner?

! An apple is a good snack.

Fetch

(FECH) *verb*

When you fetch something, you go and get it and bring it back.

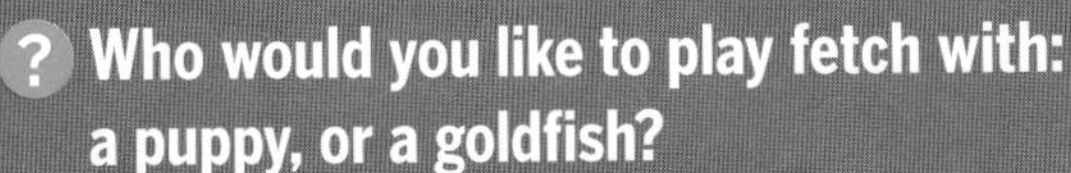

? Who would you like to play fetch with: a puppy, or a goldfish?

! A puppy. A goldfish can't fetch!

Rattle

(**RAT** – uhl) *verb*

When something rattles, it makes sharp, banging sounds.

? Which would rattle: a jar of dry beans, or a car horn?

! Dry beans rattle when you shake them.

Dwelling

(**DWEL** – ing) *noun*

A dwelling is another name for a home.

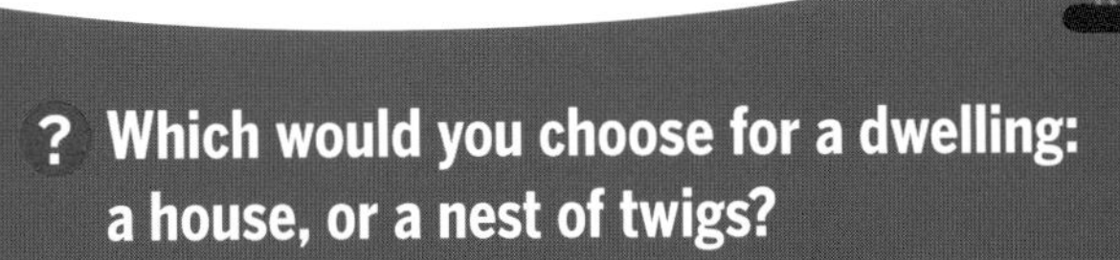

? Which would you choose for a dwelling: a house, or a nest of twigs?

! A house is a dwelling for people. Birds live in nests.

Giant

(**JIE** – uhnt) *adjective, noun*

Something giant is very big. Fairy-tale characters that are big and strong are called giants.

? Where does a giant sit when he comes over for dinner?

! Anywhere he wants!

Adventure

(ad – **VEN** – chur) *noun*

An adventure is an exciting or unusual thing that happens to you. Sometimes adventures are dangerous.

? Which sounds like a real adventure: traveling to the moon, or going to the store?

! Going to the moon. You can go to the store any day.

Flip

(**FLIP**) *verb*

If you flip something, you turn it over.

? How is a penny like a pancake?

! Both can flip!

Dawdle

(**DAW** – duhl) *verb*

5

To dawdle is to take more time than you need to go somewhere.

You'll be late! Don't dawdle!
School

? Do you dawdle when you're in a hurry?

! No. When you dawdle, you take your time.

Erase

(i – **RAYS**) *verb*

To erase is to remove something. You erase a pencil mark on your paper.

? **You erased a word on your homework. Can you read the word, or is it gone?**

! **If you erase the word, it is gone!**

Costume

(**KAHS** – toom) *noun*

A costume is what you put on to dress up as someone else. You can wear a costume to a Halloween party.

Rats! I'm wearing the wrong costume!
PHONE

? **Does a policeman wear a costume?**

! **No. A policeman wears a uniform.**

Crop

(**KRAHP**) *noun*

A crop is a group of plants, such as corn or wheat, that farmers grow for food.

? What did one crop of corn say to the other?

! Speak up! We can't "ear" you!

Hectic

(**HEK** – tik) *adjective*

When things are hectic, they are very busy and rushed.

? Is it easy to study when things are hectic?

! No. Study time is best when things are not rushed.

Cliff

(**KLIF**) *noun*

A cliff is high piece of land with a sharp, steep side.

? Where would you find a cliff: in the flat desert, or at the edge of a mountain?

! At the edge of a mountain, of course!

Nibble

(**NIB** – uhl) *verb*

When you nibble your food, you eat it in tiny bites.

? Do you take big bites when you nibble?

! No. When you nibble, you eat a little at a time.

Century

(**SEN** – chuh – ree) *noun*

A century is another way to say one hundred years.

? How long is two centuries: 120 years, or 200 years?

! 200 years equals two centuries.

Immense

9

(i – **MENS**) *adjective*

Something that is immense is really, really big.

? Is a dinosaur immense?

! Yes. It's as big as some buildings.

Liquid

(**LIK** - wid) *noun*

Liquid is something that is not solid. It can be poured. Water is a liquid.

? What did one liquid say to the other?

! You're such a drip!

Polite

10

(puh – **LIET**) *adjective*

Someone who has very good manners is polite.

? **What are two things a polite person might say?**

! **"Please" and "thank you."**

Interrupt

(in – tuh – **RUHPT**) *verb*

If you interrupt someone who is speaking, you say or do something that stops the person from talking.

? If you are talking while the teacher is talking, are you interrupting?

! Yes. Never interrupt your teacher!

Curly

(**KUR** – lee) *adjective*

Curly hair has lots of rings and curves in it.

? What's the opposite of curly hair?

! Straight hair.

Pester

(**PES** - tur) *verb*

To pester means to bother someone over and over again.

❓ **What did the ladybug say to the beetle?**

❗ **Don't pester me! Go "bug" someone else!**

Balance

(**BAL** - uhns) *noun*

People with good balance are steady on their feet.

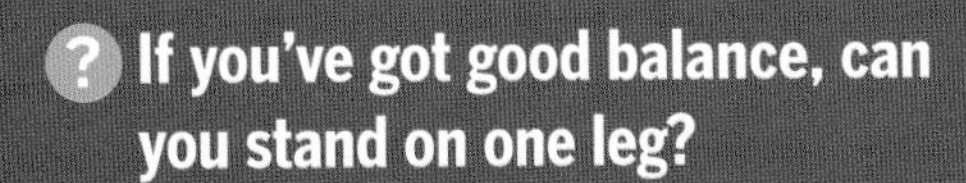

? If you've got good balance, can you stand on one leg?

! Yes. But be careful!

Meek

(**MEEK**) *adjective*

A meek person is often quiet and has a hard time speaking up for him or herself.

? Is a person who is loud and bossy meek?

! No. A meek person is not loud or bossy.

Suspicious

(suh – **SPI** – shuhs) *adjective*

If you are suspicious of someone or something, it means you don't trust them.

? If you're suspicious of someone, do you think he is going to do something nice, or naughty?

! Naughty!

Actor

(**AK** – tur) *noun*

An actor is a person who plays a character in the theater, movies or on TV.

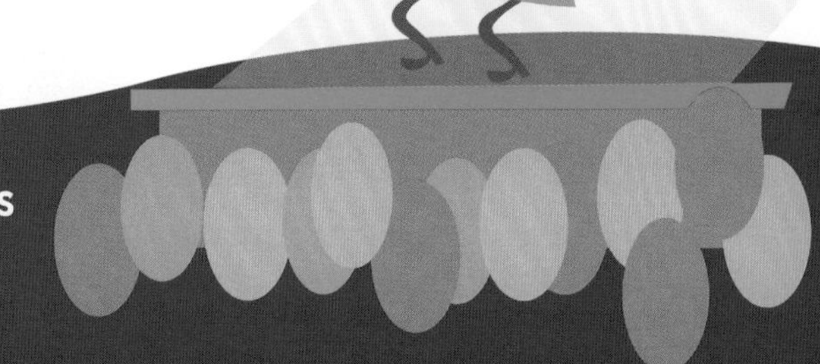

? If a baker bakes, what does an actor do?

! An actor acts.

Variety

(vuh – **RIE** – uh – tee) *noun*

14

We have a wide variety to choose from!

A variety is a choice of many different things.

? Which has more variety: a candy store, or a store that only sells black socks?

! A candy store!

Crash

(**KRASH**) *noun, verb*

A crash is when two or more things bump into each other really hard. You can also crash into something.

? What is it called when your bicycle runs into a garbage can?

! A trash crash!

Faithful

(**FAYTH** – fuhl) *adjective*

Thanks for your help. You're my most faithful friend!

If you are faithful to someone, you stand by him or her, no matter what.

? Do you leave your friend when she needs help?

! No. You're a faithful friend.

Character

(**KA** – ruhk – tur) *noun*

A character is a person in a book, cartoon, movie or TV show.

? **Does a fairy tale have characters?**

! **Yes. Fairy tales are full of fun, magical characters.**

16

Broad

(**BRAWD**) *adjective*

What broad shoulders you have!

Broad is another way to say that something is wide.

? What can you always make that will brighten someone's day?

! A broad smile!

Flood

(**FLUHD**) *noun*

A flood is when there's too much water. A river can overflow and cause a flood.

? Which is more likely to flood: land in a desert, or land near a river?

! Floods often take place by rivers.

Famous

(**FAY** – muhs) *adjective*

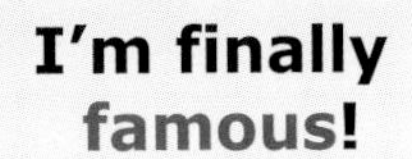

Someone or something that is very well known is famous.

? How does a scientist become famous?

! Study, study, study!

Impossible

(im – **PAHS** – uh – buhl) *adjective*

Something that is impossible can't be done, or can't happen.

? Which would you say is impossible: flying like a bird, or talking on the phone?

! Flying like a bird is impossible!

Theater

(**THEE** – uh – tur) *noun*

A theater is a place where you go to see a movie or a play.

? Which would you see at a theater: a football game, or a movie?

! A movie. A football game wouldn't fit into a theater!

Alphabet

(**AL** – fuh – bet) *noun*

The alphabet is the group of letters, A through Z, that we use to read and write.

? **Which letter comes after R in the alphabet?**

! **S, of course!**

Observe

(uhb – **ZURV**) *verb*

To observe is to watch something or someone closely.

? Where can you go to observe tigers?

! The zoo. Can you think of anywhere else?

Doughnut

(**DOH** - nuht) *noun*

A doughnut is a ring-shaped cake that is fried.

? What kind of hole is fun to get into?

! A doughnut hole!

Frown

(**FROWN**) *verb, noun*

When you frown, your mouth turns down. You make a frown when you're mad or sad.

? When is a smile like a frown?

! When you turn it upside down!

Season

(**SEE** - zuhn) *noun*

You are dressed
for the wrong season!

A season is a time of year. The four seasons are spring, summer, fall and winter.

? In which season would you build a snowman?

! Winter.

Urgent

(**UR** – juhnt) *adjective*

If something is urgent, it means it needs to be taken care of right away.

? If you cut your finger, are you in urgent need of a bandage, or a glove?

! A bandage.

Enemy

(**EN** – uh – mee) *noun*

If someone is your enemy, they don't like you.

Who is an enemy: someone who wants to harm you, or someone who wants to be your friend?

Someone who wants to harm you is your enemy.

Favorite

22

(**FAY** - vuh - ruht) *adjective*

Your favorite thing or person is the one you like the best.

? What is a spider's favorite snack?

! A piece of fly pie!

Candle

(**KAN** – duhl) *noun*

A candle is a string surrounded by wax. When you light the string, the candle burns and gives off light.

? What kind of candles are the best ones to have?

! Birthday candles!

Complain

(kuhm - **PLAYN**) *verb*

I want to complain to the cook!

People complain when they are angry or unhappy about something.

? **Should you complain about chores?**

! **No. It's important to help out.**

Porcupine

(**POR** – kyuh – pien) *noun*

A porcupine is a small woodland animal. It is covered with long, sharp spikes.

? Where might you find a porcupine: in the forest, or at the beach?

! In the forest. Porcupines don't like the beach!

Spice

(**SPIES**) *noun*

A spice is something you put on food to make it taste better. Salt and pepper are spices.

? What makes rice taste nice?

! Spice makes rice taste nice!

Brook

(**BRUK**) *noun*

A brook is a small stream.

? What might live in a brook: a frog, or a whale?

! A frog. A whale is much too big for a brook!

Interfere

(in – tur – **FEER**) *verb*

People who interfere get involved in things that are not their business.

? Can a friend interfere with your other friends?

! Yes. But a true friend tries not to!

Chimney

(**CHIM** – nee) *noun*

A chimney lets the smoke from a fireplace out of the house.

? What did one chimney say to the other?

! Don't blow your stack!

Blossom

(**BLAH** – suhm) *noun*

A blossom is the flowering part of a plant.

? Where do blossoms get their energy?

! They use flower power!

Decorate

(**DEK** – uh – rayt) *verb*

When you decorate something, you add to it to make it look prettier or special.

? How is your bedroom like a cake?

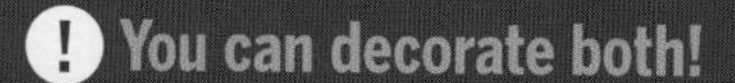

! You can decorate both!

Wander

(**WAHN** – dur) *verb*

27

Don't wander off, son...

When you wander, you walk around without planning to go to a certain place.

? **Would you wander in a race, or along a beach?**

! **Along a beach. In a race, you plan to reach the finish line.**

Mask

(**MASK**) *noun*

A mask is something you cover your face with.

? When should you wear a mask: at a costume party, or in the shower?

! At a costume party.

Pleasant

(**PLE** – zuhnt) *adjective*

Something that is pleasant is nice or enjoyable.

? **Which would be pleasant: a warm cup of hot chocolate, or a bowl of worms?**

! **Hot chocolate. A bowl of worms would be yucky!**

Earn

(**URN**) *verb*

To earn is to work for money or some other kind of reward.

? How can you earn money: by asking your mom for it, or by delivering newspapers?

! Delivering newspapers is one way to earn money.

Appetite

(**AP** – uh – tiet) *noun*

Your appetite describes how much you want to eat. An appetite can be big or small.

? Why is it bad to snack right before dinner?

! You'll ruin your appetite.

Cactus

(**KAK** – tuhs) *noun*

A cactus is a desert plant that is covered with sharp spikes.

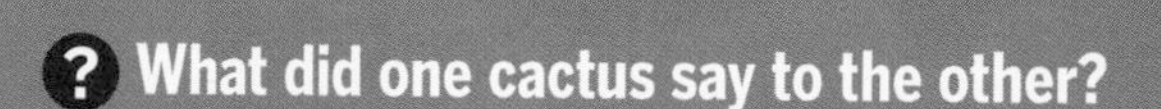

? What did one cactus say to the other?

! I'm stuck on you!

Muffin

(**MUHF** – uhn) *noun*

A muffin is a baked, sweet bread that is shaped like a cupcake.

? How many muffins are in a dozen?

! Twelve – but not for long!

Rude

(**ROOD**) *adjective*

Someone who is rude has bad manners. A rude person is not polite.

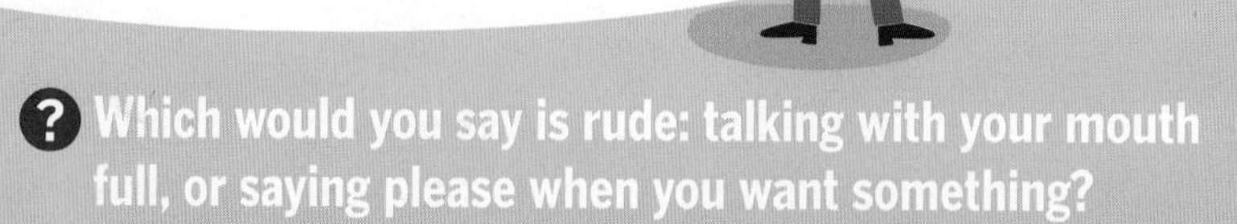

? Which would you say is rude: talking with your mouth full, or saying please when you want something?

! Talking with your mouth full is rude. Don't do it!

Shriek

(**SHREEK**) *noun, verb*

A shriek is a short, loud scream. You shriek when you are surprised or scared.

? Which would make you shriek: a snake, or a cupcake?

! A snake! HISS!

Artist

(**AHR** - tist) *noun*

An artist is a person who paints, draws, dances, makes music or does some other kind of creative work.

? **Is a ballerina an artist?**

! **Yes. Artists draw, paint, sing or dance.**

Urban

(**UR** – buhn) *adjective*

City things are described as urban.

? Do you find urban things in the woods?

! No. You find them in the city.

Forgive

(fur – **GIV**) *verb*

When you forgive someone, you stop being angry with the person for something they did.

? What are two things you can do when someone apologizes?

! Forgive and forget.

Deserve

(duh – **ZURV**) *verb*

When you deserve something, you receive it for something you have done well.

You're the best speller. You deserve a medal!
SPELLING CONTEST
1

? When do you deserve a prize: when you win a spelling contest, or when you get a flat tire?

! When you win the spelling contest.

Monument

(**MAHN** - yuh - muhnt) *noun*

A monument is a structure that honors a special person or event.

? What did the monument say to the tourist?

! Stop staring!

Curious

(**KYUR** – ee – uhs) *adjective*

If you are curious about something, you want to find out more about it.

? Would a birthday present make you curious?

! Yes. You would want to know what's inside it!

Bun

(**BUHN**) *noun*

A bun is a kind of bread. Buns can be used for hamburgers or hot dogs.

? How does a hot dog count?

! "Bun," two, three, four . . .

Scrumptious

(**SKRUHMP** – shuhs) *adjective*

35

Mmmm...
Scrumptious!

If you say your food is scrumptious, you mean that it tastes very good.

? Are flies scrumptious?

! They are if you're a frog!

Glorious

(**GLOR** – ee – uhs) *adjective*

Something that is really beautiful or very special is called glorious.

? What are some things that are glorious?

! A sunny day or a pretty flower can be glorious. Can you think of others?

Amusing

(uh – **MYOO** – zing) *adjective*

If something is amusing, it will make you laugh.

? Which is amusing: a cartoon, or a test?

! A cartoon, of course!

Pretend

(pri - **TEND**) *verb*

Pretend is another way to say that you are playing make-believe.

? Can you pretend to read?

! Yes. But reading books for real is more fun!

Fidget

(**FIJ** – it) *verb*

When you fidget, you move your body in a nervous way.

? If you fidget, are you sitting quietly?

! No. If you fidget, you move around like a monkey!

Cash

(**KASH**) *noun*

BOOKS
Take this cash and buy something nice.
$

Cash is another name for coins and paper money.

? **What kind of bank only accepts cash?**

! **A piggy bank!**

Chilly

(**CHIL** - ee) *adjective*

This snow is for the birds.

Something that is chilly feels unpleasantly cold.

? Would you be chilly sledding in the snow?

! Yes! Playing in the snow is fun, but cold.

Borrow

(**BAW** – roh) *verb*

When you borrow something from someone, you use it for a short time. Then you return it.

? Where can you borrow books?

! At the library. But remember to return them on time!

Brag

(BRAG) *verb*

I've read all of these books!

If you brag, you talk too proudly about what you have or what you have done.

? Which would you brag about: getting an "A" on a test, or having a lot of toys?

! Neither. It is not polite to brag.

Feather

(**FE*TH*** – ur) *noun*

Feathers cover a bird's body.

? **If something isn't heavy at all, what is it?**

! **Light as a feather!**

Remarkable

(ri – **MAHR** – kuh – buhl) *adjective*

When something is remarkable, it is very special.

? Is lifting a bus remarkable?

! Yes. It's something only super heroes can do!

WOW! That's remarkable!

Neighbor

(**NAY** – bur) *noun*

A neighbor is someone who lives in a house nearby.

? Are your parents your neighbors?

! No. Neighbors live nearby, not in the same house.

Expensive

(ek – **SPEN** – siv) *adjective*

When something costs a lot of money, it is called expensive.

? Why does a skunk think everything is expensive?

! Because he only has a few "scents"!

Ladder

(**LAD** - ur) *noun*

A ladder has steps or rungs. You climb a ladder so you can reach up high.

? **What did the house say to the ladder?**

! **You can lean on me!**

Luggage

(**LUH** – gij) *noun*

Luggage is what you carry your things in when you travel.

Which animal is never without luggage?

An elephant. He always has his trunk!

Brownie

(**BROWN** – ee) *noun*

A brownie is a baked chocolate dessert.

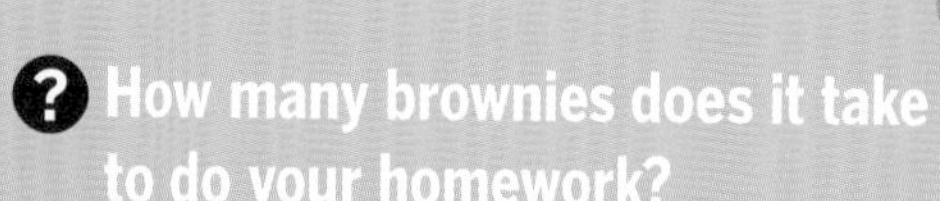

? **How many brownies does it take to do your homework?**

! **None. But one would sure be sweet!**

Exit

(**EG** - zit) *noun*

Exit is the door you go through to get out of a building.

? What is the polite thing to say to an elephant as you walk toward an exit?

! After you!

Elevator

(**E** – luh – vay – tur) *noun*

An elevator is a machine that carries people up and down floors in a tall building.

? Is an elevator always in a good mood?

! No. Sometimes it's up, sometimes it's down!

Contest

(**KAHN** – test) *noun*

A contest is a race or game people enter with the hope of winning a prize.

? What kind of contest can you never lose?

! The race to do your very best!

Hive

(**HIEV**) *noun*

A hive is a nest for bees.

What do you do before you enter a hive?

Ring the "buzz"-er!

Thunderstorm

(**THUHN** – dur – storm) *noun*

A thunderstorm is a big rainstorm that has loud thunder and bright lightning.

? Why do fireflies like thunderstorms?

! Because they're lightning bugs!

Instrument

(**IN** – struh – muhnt) *noun*

A musical instrument is something you use to make music.

? What musical instrument do you always have with you?

! Your whistle!

Middle

(**MI** – duhl) *noun*

Something that is in the middle is in between other things.

Where's the monkey?
In the middle!

There are three children in a family. When was the one in the middle born?

The one in the middle was born second, of course!

Flash

(**FLASH**) *noun*

A flash is a quick burst of bright light.

Which flashes: thunder, or lightning?

Lightning flashes.

Tremble

(**TREM** – buhl) *verb*

To tremble is to shake from fear or cold.

Why do you tremble after a day of playing in the snow?

Because it's cold. Brrrr!

Refrigerator

(ri – **FRIJ** – uh – ray – tur) *noun*

A refrigerator is a large container that makes cold air. The cold air inside refrigerators keeps food fresh.

? What does a refrigerator do all day?

! Nothing. It just "chills" out!

Perform

(pur – **FORM**) *verb*

If you perform a dance or a song, you do it to entertain people.

? Would you like to perform in a circus, or in a school play?

! Some may say circus, some may say school play. Both are correct!

Bubble

(**BUH** – buhl) *noun*

A bubble is a pocket of air inside a thin skin. Soap and chewing gum make bubbles.

? Which makes better bubbles: mashed potatoes, or soapy water?

! Soapy water. Mashed potatoes make terrible bubbles!

Crust

(**KRUHST**) *noun*

I love eating
the crust first!

The crust is the outside edge of something. Pies and bread have a crust.

? What is true about pizza and pie?

! Their crust is a must!

Firefly

(**FIER** – flie) *noun*

A firefly is a bug that makes light with its body.

? What did the firefly say to his girlfriend?

! You light up my life!

Insect

(**IN** – sekt) *noun*

An insect is a name for a kind of bug. Flies and mosquitoes are insects.

? Which is an insect: an ant, or an antelope?

! An ant. An antelope is a kind of deer!

Dare

(**DAYR**) *verb*

Do I dare jump?

To dare to do something is to bravely take a chance. You can also dare someone else to do something.

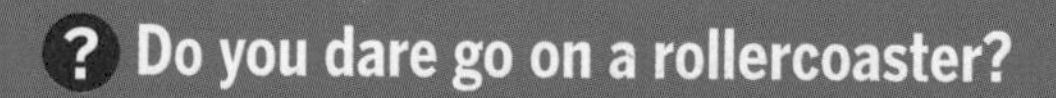

? Do you dare go on a rollercoaster?

! Yes. But only if you're allowed.

Vanish

(**VA** – nish) *verb*

To vanish is to disappear, or go away, suddenly.

? Do you want to make an ice cream cone vanish?

! Yes! But only if you get to eat it!

Bewildered

(bi – **WIL** – durd) *adjective*

If you are bewildered, you don't understand what is going on.

? What should you do if you are bewildered in school?

! Ask your teacher for help.

Astronaut

(**AS** – truh – naht) *noun*

An astronaut explores outer space.

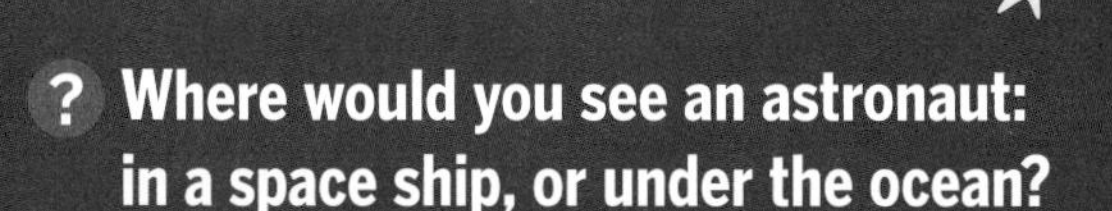

? Where would you see an astronaut: in a space ship, or under the ocean?

! Astronauts explore space, not the sea!

Authority

(uh – **THOR** – uh – tee) *noun*

Authority is the power to do something or the power to tell others what to do.

? Can you name four people who have authority?

! Yes! Your parents, a policeman, a fireman and a teacher. Try to think of more!

Blizzard

(**BLI** - zurd) *noun*

A blizzard is a big storm that has heavy snow and strong winds.

? Would you wear your bathing suit in a blizzard?

! No! You would wear your coat and hat.

Appointment

148

(uh – **POINT** – muhnt) *noun*

I'm here for our breakfast appointment!

An appointment is a plan to meet someone at a certain time and place.

? How is an appointment like a promise?

! You should always keep both.

Quarrel

(**KWAW** – ruhl) *verb, noun*

To quarrel is to argue. A quarrel is another name for an argument.

? Do you like to quarrel?

! No! It's better to play with your friends, not fight with them.

Ancient

(**AYN** - shunt) *adjective*

Something that is ancient is from a long, long time ago.

? Which would you say is ancient: your lunch, or an old mummy?

! An old mummy. Don't ever eat an ancient lunch!

Hasty

(**HAY** – stee) *adjective*

Hasty means that you do something a little too fast.

? If you are hasty when you paint, what will happen?

! You will make a big mess!

Advantage

(ad – **VAN** – tij) *noun*

If you have an advantage, it means you have a better chance at something.

? What is the best way to get an advantage on a test?

! Pay attention in class.

Bucket

(**BUH** - kit) *noun*

A bucket is a round container with a handle. It can also be called a pail.

? You can catch a ball. What can a bucket catch?

! Rain!

Positive

(**PAHZ** – uh – tiv) *adjective*

If you are positive about something, it means that you are sure that it is right.

? What three things should you be positive about when you leave home?

! Your name, your address and your phone number.

Budge

(**BUHJ**) *verb*

When you budge something, you move it just a little.

? Could you use fudge to make your friend budge?

! Yes, if she liked chocolate!

Chirp

(**CHURP**) *noun, verb*

A chirp is a small, sharp sound. Birds and bugs chirp.

? Which might make a chirp: a puppy, or a cricket?

! A cricket chirps. Puppies bark!

Private

(**PRIE** - vit) *adjective*

Something private is for you and no one else. Places and thoughts can be private.

? Would you want your birthday to be private?

! No! You would want to invite all your friends to a party.

Afford

(uh - **FORD**) *verb*

If you can afford something, it means you have enough money to buy it.

? What gift can you always afford to give?

! A smile!

Relax

(ri – **LAKS**) *verb*

When you relax, you feel calm and rested.

? How would you like to relax: by going to the playground, or by taking a nap?

! You relax when you take a nap.

Accept

(ak – **SEPT**) *verb*

Will you come to my party?
Yes, I accept your invitation.

To accept something means to take it or agree to it.

? **What do you say when your friend offers you a ripe, juicy peach?**

! **I accept!**

Wink

(**WINGK**) *verb*

When you wink, you quickly close and open one eye. You can wink at someone to send a message.

? **Would you wink at a friend or at a person you don't know?**

! **You should only wink at friends. Don't wink at strangers.**

Trickle

(**TRIK** – uhl) *verb*

Trickle means to fall slowly, in little drops. Water can trickle.

? What might trickle water?

! A leaky faucet.

Immediately

61

(i – **MEE** – dee – it – lee) *adverb*

When I feed Spot,
he comes immediately!
SPOT

If something happens immediately, it happens right away.

? When your teacher asks you a question, do you answer immediately?

! Yes! You answer questions right away.

Journey

(**JUR** – nee) *noun*

A journey is a long trip.

? Which would you say is a journey: a trip across America, or a walk across the room?

! A trip across America is a nice, long journey!

Celebrate

(**SE** – luh – brayt) *verb*

To celebrate means to make something special. You can celebrate your birthday.

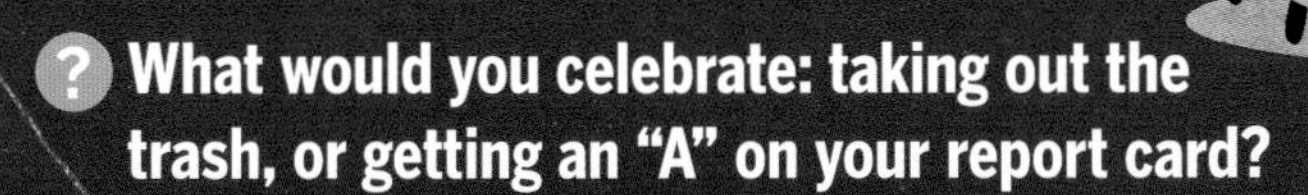

? What would you celebrate: taking out the trash, or getting an “A” on your report card?

! Getting an “A”. Good job!

Puff

(**PUHF**) *noun*

A puff is a little cloud of something, like smoke.

How is a campfire like a dragon?

Both make puffs of smoke.

Swarm

(**SWORM**) *noun*

A swarm is a big cloud of flying insects, such as bees or flies.

? Which would you rather see: a swarm of bees, or a swarm of flies?

! Flies. At least they don't sting!

Dismal

(**DIZ** - muhl) *adjective*

Something that is dismal makes you sad.

? **What should you do if your friend feels dismal?**

! **Cheer them up! That's what friends are for.**

Voyage

(**VOI** – ij) *noun*

A voyage is a long trip.

? Which voyage sounds like more fun: a trip to a pretty island, or a trip to the grocery store?

! A pretty island sounds fun. Let's go!

Litter

(**LIT** - ur) *noun*

Litter is trash that has been thrown on the ground.

? When is trash not litter?

! When it is in a trash can.

Diary

(**DIE** - uh - ree) *noun*

You write your private thoughts in a diary.

? Would you let someone read your diary?

! No! It's just for you.

Odor

(**OH** - dur) *noun*

An odor is a strong smell. It usually doesn't smell very good.

? What finger on a skunk's hand has the strongest odor?

! His stinky pinky!

Tumble

(**TUHM** – buhl) *verb*

To tumble is to roll and bounce. Sometimes when you fall, you tumble.

? Can it be fun to tumble?

! Yes. A somersault is a kind of tumble.

Oaf

(**OHF**) *noun*

An oaf is a big, clumsy person.

? **How do you make a clumsy sandwich?**

! **Use an "oaf" of bread!**

Mutter

(**MUHT** - ur) *verb*

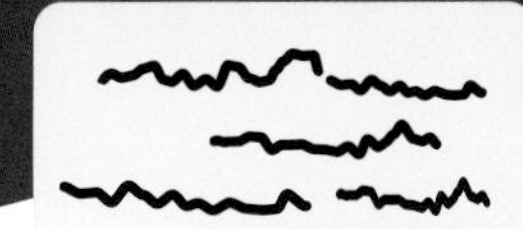

When you mutter, you speak softly and people can't hear you.

? **Your friend mutters. Do you ask him to speak more quietly, or to speak up?**

! **Speak up, please!**

Mountain

(**MOWN** – tuhn) *noun*

I'm king of the mountain!

A mountain is a very high hill with steep sides.

? Can a mountain be flat?

! No. Mountains are very tall hills.

Weep

(**WEEP**) *verb*

To weep means to cry.

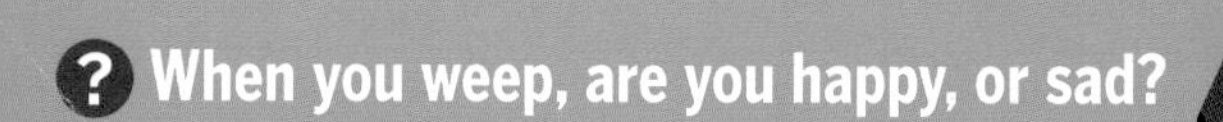

? When you weep, are you happy, or sad?

! You weep when you're sad.

Average

(**A** – vrij) *adjective*

Something that is average is normal or ordinary.

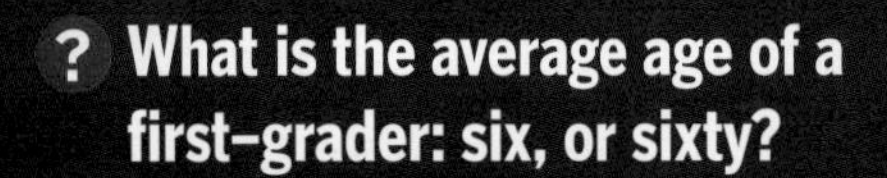

? **What is the average age of a first-grader: six, or sixty?**

! **The average first-grader is six years old.**

Cattle

(**KAT** - uhl) *noun*

Cattle are cows and bulls.

? **Where would you find cattle: in a grassy field, or riding on an airplane?**

! **Cows like grassy fields.**

Autumn

(**AW** – tuhm) *noun*

Autumn is the season between summer and winter. It is also called fall.

? **What do leaves do in autumn?**

! **They "fall"!**

Umbrella

(uhm – **BRE** – luh) *noun*

An umbrella is used to protect you from the rain and sun.

? Would you use an umbrella in the shower?

! No! Umbrellas are for outside only, please.

Knowledge

(**NAH** – lij) *noun*

LIBRARY
Knowledge is tasty!

To have knowledge is to know and understand something.

? How is knowledge like a fish?

! You can find it in a school.

Correct

(kuh – **REKT**) *adjective*

If something is correct, it has no mistakes.

? Which is correct: 2 + 2 = 4, or 3 + 3 = 7?

! 2 + 2 = 4 is correct.

Hollow

(**HAH** – loh) *adjective*

If something is hollow, it is empty inside. It is not solid.

? Which might be hollow: a rock, or an old tree?

! An old tree. Most rocks aren't hollow!

Valuable

(**VAL** – yuh – buhl) *adjective*

Something that is valuable is worth a lot of money, or is important to you.

? Which do you think is more valuable: a gold ring, or a paper ring?

! A gold ring is more valuable.

Poison

(**POI** – zuhn) *noun*

A poison **can cause harm to living things.** Poison **is very dangerous.**

What should you always do if you find something marked "poison"?

Don't touch it! Go tell a grown-up.

Opinion

(uh – **PIN** – yuhn) *noun*

An opinion is a strong feeling about something.

? You think chocolate ice cream is tasty. Is that an opinion?

! Yes. But your friend's opinion is that vanilla tastes best.

Attention

(uh - **TEN** - shuhn) *noun*

When you pay attention to something, you focus your mind on it.

? What can you pay that doesn't cost you money?

! You can pay attention!

Wagon

(**WA** – guhn) *noun*

A wagon is a small cart with a handle and wheels.

? How is a wagon like a bicycle?

! They both have wheels. But you can only pedal a bicycle.

Wrinkled

(**RING** – kuhld) *adjective*

Something that has a lot of lines and folds is called wrinkled. Cloth is something that can be wrinkled.

? **Which might be wrinkled: an old paper bag, or a basketball?**

! **An old paper bag.**

Vacation

(vay - **KAY** - shuhn) *noun*

A vacation is a break from school or work.

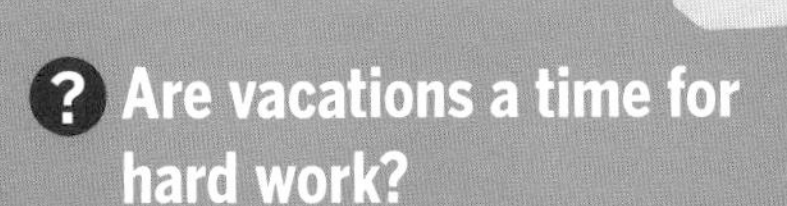

? Are vacations a time for hard work?

! No! Vacation is a time to relax and have fun.

Exclaim

(eks – **KLAYM**) *verb*

To exclaim is to suddenly speak loudly and strongly.

? What might you exclaim at a surprise party?

! Happy Birthday!

Fancy

(**FAN** – see) *adjective*

Something that is fancy is special and not ordinary or plain.

? Which do you think is fancy: a T-shirt and jeans, or a suit and tie?

! A suit and tie are very fancy.

Tangle

(**TANG** – guhl) *noun, verb*

A tangle is a mess of knots. You can also tangle something, like string.

? How is your hair like the string of a kite?

! Both can get tangled. Ouch!

Treasure

(**TRE** - zhur) *noun*

A treasure is a collection of expensive things such as jewelry or gold.

? Which would you call treasure: a bag of gold, or a bag of stinky socks?

! A bag of gold is a treasure. A bag of stinky socks is laundry.

Collection

(kuh - **LEK** - shuhn) *noun*

A collection is a group of one kind of thing. You can have a collection of seashells or stamps.

? How is a stamp collection like a lollipop?

! Both get licked!

Peculiar

(pi – **KYOOL** – yur) *adjective*

Something peculiar is very strange.

? Which would you say is peculiar: a cat with wings, or a dog with a tail?

! A cat with wings is very peculiar!

Surround

(suh - **ROWND**) *verb*

To surround means to circle something on all sides.

? **Could you surround a yard with a fence? Yes, or no?**

! **Yes. Good job!**

Expect

(ek – **SPEKT**) *verb*

When you expect something, you think it will happen.

? What do you expect when the sky is gray and cloudy?

! Rain, rain, rain!

Invent

(in – **VENT**) *verb*

When you invent something, you are the first person to think of, or make, that thing.

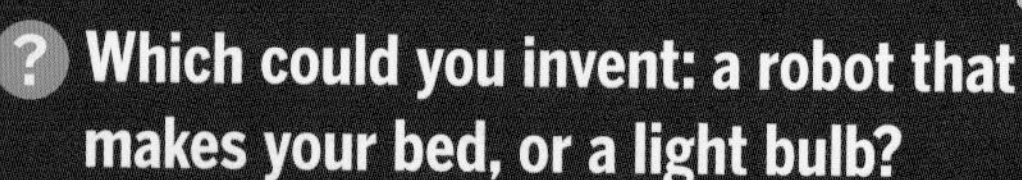

? Which could you invent: a robot that makes your bed, or a light bulb?

! A robot that makes the bed. The light bulb has already been invented!

Ribbon

(**RI** - buhn) *noun*

A ribbon is a thin strip of cloth. You can tie your hair or packages with ribbon.

? What would you tie with ribbon: a birthday present, or your ham sandwich?

! Presents get ribbons. Ham sandwiches get eaten!

Alarm

(uh - **LAHRM**) *noun*

An alarm is a loud sound, or a flashing light. It can wake you, or warn you.

? **How is a rooster like an alarm clock?**

! **Both wake you up early. Cock - a - doodle - do!**

Suds

(**SUHDZ**) *noun*

Suds are the bubbles that soap and water make.

? **Where can you find suds?**

! **Suds are in a bathroom, a sink and a washing machine. Can you think of other places?**

Island

(**IE** – luhnd) *noun*

An island is land that is completely circled by water.

? Which state is made up of only islands?

! Hawaii. Aloha!

Guest

(**GEST**) *noun*

Someone who is visiting your house is called a guest.

? Are your parents guests?

! No. They live in your house. They're not visitors.

Recent

(**REE** – suhnt) *adjective*

There must have been a recent rain!

Something that is recent happened a little while ago.

? Which of these events is recent: lunch today, or your first birthday?

! Lunch today is more recent.

Sprinkle

(**SPRING** – kuhl) *verb*

Sprinkle means to spread around small bits of things.

? Which would you sprinkle on a cupcake: sugar, or salt?

! You would sprinkle sugar on a cupcake. You would sprinkle salt on potatoes. Yum!

Gloomy

(**GLOOM** – ee) *adjective*

A place that is dark can be called gloomy. If you are sad, you can also say that you feel gloomy.

? Which day of the week is never gloomy?

! Sun-day!

Entrance

(**EN** - truhns) *noun*

An entrance is the way into a room or a building.

? Do you like to look for the exit at an amusement park?

! No! You want to go in the entrance and never leave!

Curve

(**KURV**) *noun, verb*

I wish I could hit the curve ball!

A curve is a line that bends.
A road can also curve.

? Where would you find a curve: on a square, or on a circle?

! On a circle, of course!

Pause

(**PAWZ**) *verb*

When you pause while doing something, you stop for a short time.

? Is a nap like a pause?

! Not really. A nap is a long rest. A pause is a short break.

Squawk

(**SKWAWK**) *noun, verb*

A squawk is a loud, harsh scream. Some large birds squawk.

? **Which animal squawks: a cow, or a big parrot?**

! **A parrot. Cows moo.**

Reward

(ri – **WORD**) *noun*

Here's your reward for finding Fifi!

A reward is a prize you are given for doing something good and special.

? Which deserves a reward: returning a lost bike, or keeping a bike you found?

! Returning the bike! Always return what doesn't belong to you.

Cheetah

(**CHEE** – tuh) *noun*

A cheetah is a wild cat with black spots that lives in Africa and Asia. A cheetah can run very fast.

? Why did the big cat have to stay after school?

! He was a "cheetah"!

Habit

(**HAB** - it) *noun*

A habit is something you do very often without thinking about it. A habit can be good or bad.

? You cover your mouth when you cough. Is that a good habit?

! Yes! Not covering your mouth when you cough is a bad habit.

Juggle

(**JUHG** – uhl) *verb*

To juggle is to toss and keep many things in the air at the same time.

? Which can you juggle: soup, or tomatoes?

! Tomatoes! Soup is too messy to juggle!

Squeak

(**SKWEEK**) *noun, verb*

A squeak is a short, high noise. To squeak is to make that noise.

? Which makes a squeak: a mouse, or a lion?

! A mouse squeaks. A lion roars. Grrr!

Chuckle

(**CHUH** – kuhl) *verb*

Chuckle means to laugh quietly.

? What makes you chuckle: silly things, or sad things?

! Silly things make you laugh.

Steep

(**STEEP**) *adjective*

I love a steep climb!

A steep hill rises and falls sharply. It is hard to go up a steep slope or stairs.

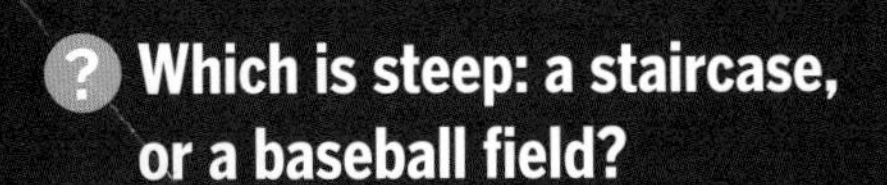

? Which is steep: a staircase, or a baseball field?

! A staircase is steep. A baseball field is flat.

Announce

(uh – **NOWNS**) *verb*

I'd like to announce the winners.
TALENT DAY

To announce is to say something important to a group of people.

? What would you announce: the winner of a race, or a friend's secret?

! The winner of a race. Don't announce a friend's secret!

Burst

(**BURST**) *verb*

To burst is to suddenly break open.

? Which can burst: a balloon, or an apple?

! A balloon. Kaboom!

Carnival

(**KAHR** – nuh – vuhl) *noun*

A carnival is a festival with food, music and dancing.

? What would you do at a carnival: eat cotton-candy, or watch TV?

! Eat cotton-candy – but not too much!

Opposite

(**AH** - puh - zit) *adjective*

Opposite describes things that are very different from each other. Night is the opposite of day.

? What is the opposite of hot?

! Cold is the opposite of hot.

Glossy

(**GLAWS** – ee) *adjective*

Something that is glossy is smooth and shiny.

? How is a shiny new car like a slippery wet fish?

! Both look glossy!

Comfortable

(**KUHM** – fur – tuh – buhl) *adjective*

Comfortable describes something that feels good to you. Soft, fuzzy slippers are comfortable.

? Who finds a pile of rocks comfortable?

! A snake sleeping in the sun.

Doodle

(**DOO** – duhl) *noun, verb*

A doodle is a simple drawing. When you doodle, you draw without thinking too much.

? Is a photo a doodle?

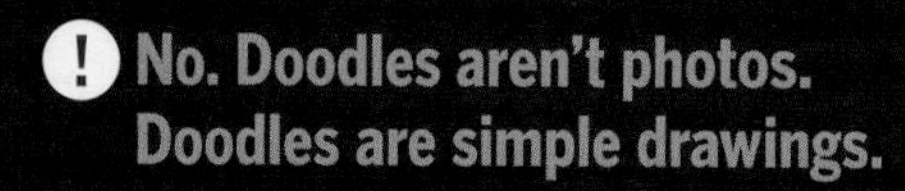

! No. Doodles aren't photos. Doodles are simple drawings.

Fortune

(**FOR** – chuhn) *noun*

A fortune is a large amount of money and wealth.

? How are toys like a fortune?

! They are fun to have and easy to lose!

Bland

(**BLAND**) *adjective*

Something that is bland is dull and plain.

? Which is bland: a piece of dry toast, or a spicy taco?

! Dry toast. A spicy taco is not bland!

Narrow

(**NA** – roh) *adjective*

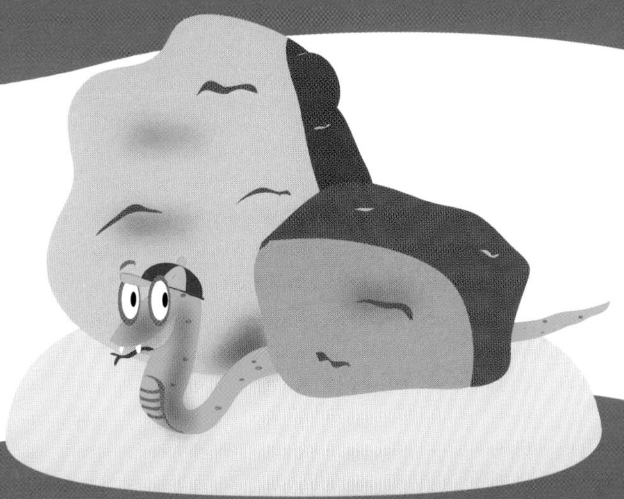

Something that is not very wide is narrow.

? Which of these sounds narrow: a basketball hoop, a straw or a dinosaur's mouth?

! A straw is most narrow.

Imagination

(i – maj – uh – **NAY** – shuhn) *noun*

Imagination is the power to make up pictures or stories that appear only in your mind.

? How often should you use your imagination?

! Every day. Imagination is fun!

Adopt

(uh – **DAHPT**) *verb*

To adopt is to take in and treat as your own. Parents can adopt a child.

? Can you adopt a stray dog?

! Yes. You would treat him as your own.

Talent

(**TA** – luhnt) *noun*

A talent is a special thing that you are good at.

? Which is a talent: playing the piano, or eating breakfast?

! Playing the piano. But breakfast is important.

Peel

(**PEEL**) *verb, noun*

To peel is to take the skin off of something. A peel is also the skin of some fruits and vegetables.

? Do you eat banana peels?

! No. You peel them off and eat what's inside.

Faint

(**FAYNT**) *adjective*

Faint describes something that is weak, like a faraway sound.

Which would make a faint sound: a tiny bird peeping, or a big dog barking?

A tiny bird would make a faint peep.

Cozy

(**KOH** - zee) *adjective*

Something cozy is pleasant and comfortable.

? **Who would find the bottom of the sea cozy?**

! **Fish feel very comfortable in the sea.**

Sturdy

(**STUR** – dee) *adjective*

These shelves are sturdy! Those shelves are not!

Something that is sturdy is strong and steady.

? Which is sturdy: a brand new chair, or an old broken stool?

! A chair. You would sit there.

Parade

(puh – **RAYD**) *noun*

When people celebrate by marching through town, it's called a parade.

? What can you find in a calendar and a parade?

! March!

Gawk

(**GAWK**) *verb*

When you gawk at someone or something, you stare at them in a rude or stupid way.

? Would you gawk at a monkey on a bicycle, or a bird in a tree?

! A monkey on a bicycle. That's very strange.

Agree

(uh - **GREE**) *verb*

To agree is to feel the same way about something.

? Do you always agree with your friends?

! No, but it's okay to have different opinions.

Glance

(**GLANS**) *verb*

To glance is to take a quick look at something or someone.

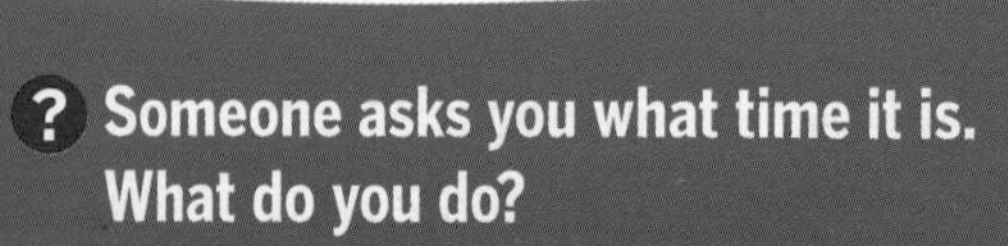

? Someone asks you what time it is. What do you do?

! Glance at your watch.

Crisp

(**KRISP**) *adjective*

Something that is firm and crunchy is called crisp.

? Is apple sauce crisp?

! No, but it sure is tasty!

Crackle

(**KRAK** – uhl) *verb*

When something crackles, it makes many small, sharp noises.

? How are some cereals like fireworks?

! They crackle – pop, pop, pop!

Index

Copyright © 2007 by Play Bac Publishing USA, Inc.

All rights reserved. No portion of this book may be
reproduced mechanically, electronically, or by
any other means, including photocopying, without
written permission of the publisher.

ISBN-13: 978-1-60214-003-5

Play Bac Publishing USA, Inc.
225 Varick Street
New York, NY 10014-4381

Printed in Malaysia

Distributed by
Black Dog & Leventhal Publishers, Inc.
151 West 19th Street
New York, NY 10011

First printing, January 2007